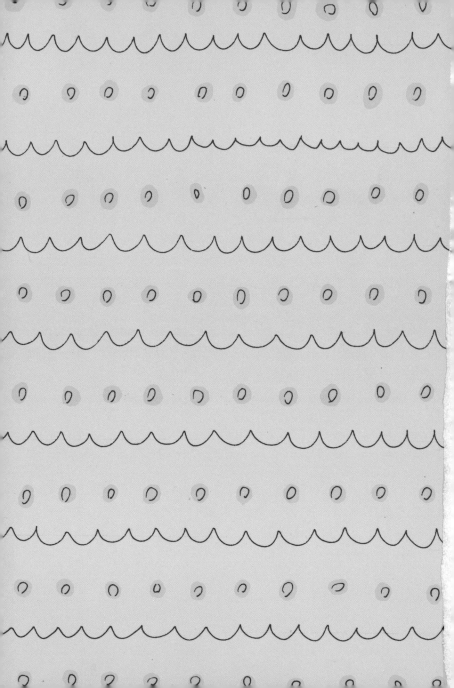

Why Don't You Write My Eulogy Now So I Can Correct It?

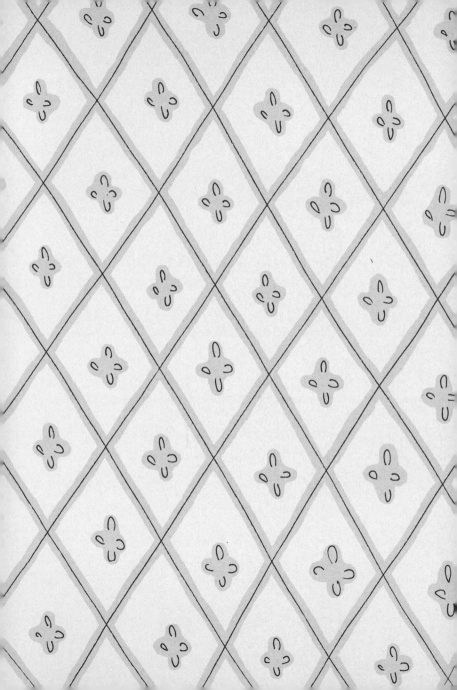

Why Don't You Write My Eulogy Now So I Can Correct It?

A MOTHER'S SUGGESTIONS

Patricia Marx

Illustrated by
Roz Chast

CELADON BOOKS, NEW YORK

www.celadonbooks.com

Cover design by Anne Twomey

Cover illustrations by Roz Chast

ISBN 978-1-250-30196-3 (hardcover)
ISBN 978-1-250-30197-0 (ebook)

Our books may be purchased in bulk for promotional, educational, or business use. Please contact your local bookseller or the Macmillan Corporate and Premium Sales Department at 1-800-221-7945, extension 5442, or by email at MacmillanSpecialMarkets@macmillan.com.

First Edition: April 2019

10 9 8 7 6 5 4 3 2 1

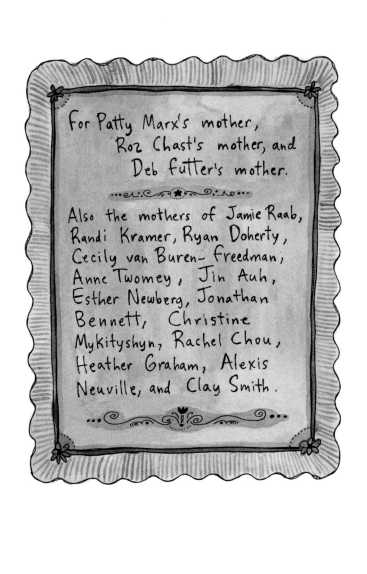

For Patty Marx's mother,
    Roz Chast's mother, and
        Deb Futter's mother.

Also the mothers of Jamie Raab,
Randi Kramer, Ryan Doherty,
Cecily van Buren-Freedman,
Anne Twomey, Jin Auh,
Esther Newberg, Jonathan
Bennett, Christine
Mykityshyn, Rachel Chou,
Heather Graham, Alexis
Neuville, and Clay Smith.

Introduction

My mother is an absolutist. Wait—is that the right word? My mother is not Louis XIV.

But she does believe in absolute rules:

A little background, but not too much: My mother was born in Philadelphia and so were her parents. Before that is anyone's guess.

My mother has no interest in the past other than regretting it.

When I was a baby, my father used to stand over my crib and read *The New York Times* to me. As soon as I stopped with the baby talk and was capable enough in English, he taught me how to read, and then gave me books unsuitable for my age. (How old were you when you read *The Tin Drum*, the story about a three-year-old who decides to stop growing, as told by his adult self in a mental asylum? I was eight.)

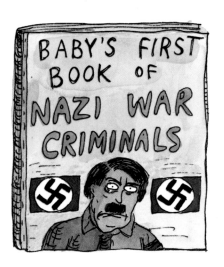

This book isn't about my father, though, so let me tell you that while my father was reading to me about the execution of Julius and Ethel Rosenberg, I do not know what my mother was doing. Neither does she. "I'm not sure I was there," she said half-kidding when I asked what I was like as a baby. "But you were perfect," she added with conviction. "You were the first child in America to wear French clothes." Obviously, that is not true. Thomas Jefferson traveled to Paris in the 1700s and you can bet the Monticello plantation that he brought back magnificent frocks for his friends' children.

When I was in second grade, I informed my mother that I had decided to run away. She packed me a lunch and said goodbye. "You can go anywhere you want," she told me, "as long as you don't cross the street."

Mary Poppins my mother was not. "If you ever have children, don't let me babysit," she advised me years later, and then explained: "Today in Toys 'R' Us, I managed to lose not just one but two children." She was referring to my niece and nephew, then about seven and four. "I wasn't worried," she added, "because I figured that they were together and had each other."

From my mother, I learned to always think of others. I phrased it that way to make you think that my mother imbued me with the value of charity and the significance of civic duty. This is how I should have put it: She acutely cared what other people thought of us, even if nobody was paying attention. "When Daddy and I come up for Parents' Weekend," my mother wrote to me one summer I was at overnight camp (I was nine), "you are to stop whatever you are doing and run up and hug us. Even if you are in the middle of a tennis match. It's too embarrassing to be the only parents whose daughter doesn't miss them."

My mother would have been a terrific five-star general or air traffic controller, but in those days, women did not have careers. Also, she had car-pool obligations.

For a few years she was a guidance counselor in an inner-city school for girls. "This gives me the opportunity to ruin not just three lives, but hundreds," she said.

My mother was great at getting girls into top colleges—especially girls who came from what were then called "broken homes." She knew the trick. All recommendations had to contain the magic word:

One year when I came home from college during spring break, there was a girl sleeping in my bed. Her mother was an alcoholic, her father had abandoned her. In the fall, thanks to my mother, she would be going to Harvard on a full scholarship paid for by the Coast Guard. Also thanks to my mother, she had a wardrobe from Bonwit Teller. The following spring, the girl dropped out of Harvard.

By the way, when I went away to college, my mother sewed name tags into my underpants. We both thought college was overnight camp, but more expensive.

My mother quit being a guidance counselor because she didn't like having a job that did not allow her to be on the phone whenever she wanted.

On the topic of sex, my mother had nothing to say and neither do I.

For many years, my mother worked alongside my father, co-running Marx Office Supplies. Needless to say, the Marx house was stocked with lots of paper, pens, Magic Markers, hole punches, gold stars, and adhesive labels that said Hello, My Name Is.

My mother and father met on the beach at Atlantic City. On their thirty-fifth anniversary, my parents' friends threw them a surprise party. My mother found out about the celebration a few days beforehand and instructed my brother, sister, and me on what clothes to wear.

My brother and sister made a collage with photos of my parents to display at the party. In the center of the poster board was a picture of a smiling young couple on the beach at Atlantic City in the 1940s. The man, my father, had his arm around the woman, my—whoops. That woman was not my mother.

My point is that back then, all women and all bathing suits looked alike.

Anyway, my parents had a happy and long marriage.

My father once told me that if my mother died before he did, he would stay in his bedroom for the rest of his life. Partly this was because without my mother, he would not know what to wear or eat.

My father thought my mother looked like the actress Jacqueline Bisset.

My mother thought my father should put on a different shirt. "The only men who can get away with short-sleeved button-downs are butchers," she said.

My mother is a wellspring of certainty about what you should do, say, wear, and believe. And when she doesn't know, she knows what to do. She calls her friend Nancy.

My mother never hesitates to say what other mothers would not even think to think. She calls it constructive criticism. Let me amend that. To her friends, my mother is sympathetic and supportive. To strangers, she is gracious and considerate. In the company of me, or for that matter my sister or brother, my mother does not beat around the bush.

When I was thirty, living rent-free at the home of my best friend and her husband, spending months trying to write the Great American Novel but getting only as far as the So-So American Sentence, my mother left a message on my phone machine that said, "There are four reasons you depress me. 1) no job 2) no apartment 3) no boyfriend. I'll call you back when I remember the fourth."

Years later, after I began to have occasional magazine articles published, she told me, "Guess what?! I didn't like your piece in *Time*, but if enough people like it, I'll change my mind."

I know what you're thinking. How demoralizing! How could a parent be so unabashedly blunt? Hasn't your mother heard about unconditional love? Probably not, but anyway, here's the thing. There is a lot to be said for knowing you are not being lied to.

Here, then, is the truth. As my mother sees it.

I apologize if this little book ends abruptly and lacks a plot or tension or more words. I blame, as always, my mother. Whenever I began to relate a story that had to do with me, she'd interrupt. "Just tell me," she'd say anxiously, "is it good for you or bad for you?"

Why Don't You Write My Eulogy Now So I Can Correct It?

Humming is hostile.

Plan every detail of your dinner party months in advance.
The table should be set days ahead of the event.

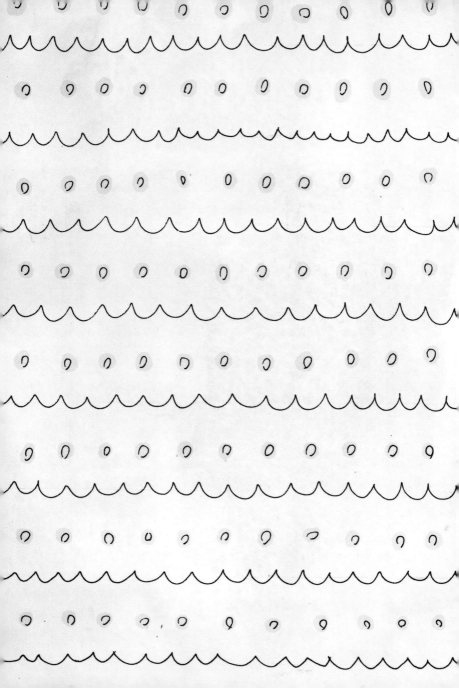

If you run out of food at your dinner party,
the world will end.

Even so, don't go overboard in the number of dishes you serve or your table will look like a Las Vegas buffet.

Girls named Susan are full of confidence.

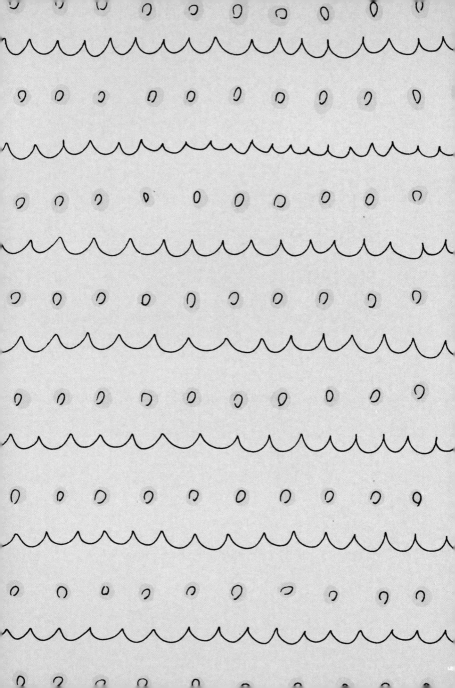

Pack a raincoat.

You don't need to spend much time in San Francisco.
It's all frosting and no cake.

If you use "me" or "him" ungrammatically, people
will think I did a bad job bringing you up.

Nature, if seen at all, is best seen from a car.

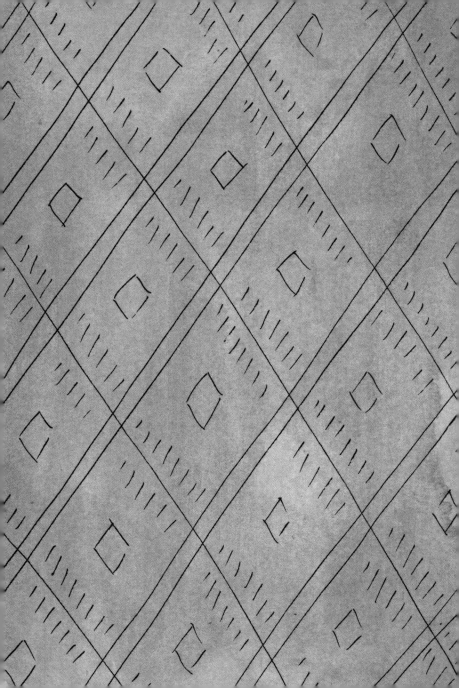

Never do anything you can pay someone else to do.

When traveling, call the hotel from the airport to say there aren't enough towels in your room and, by the way, you'd like a room with a better view.

If your book club chooses *Absalom, Absalom!*,
that will be the end of your book club.

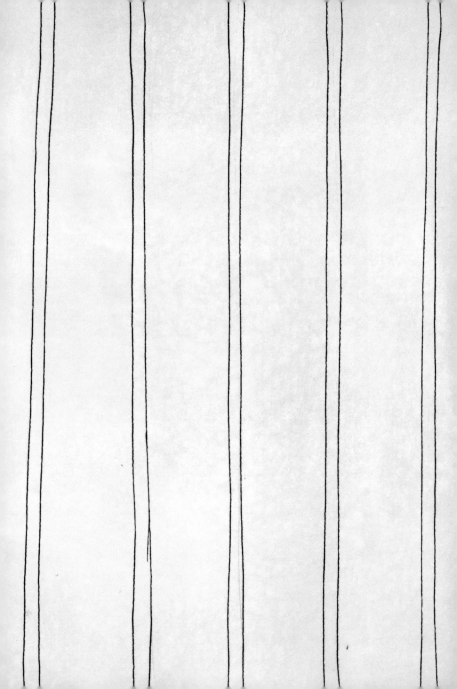

Don't bring dessert to a dinner party. The host
does not want to put your Carvel Fudgie the
Whale ice cream on the table next to the dessert
she spent three days preparing.

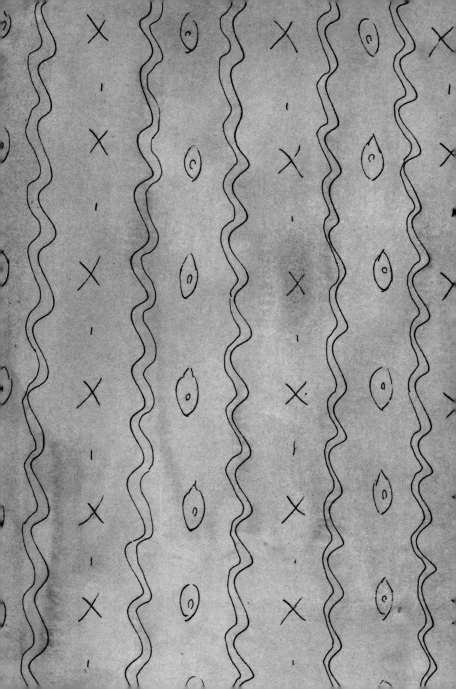

Avoid sleeves that have names unless
you are in a theatrical production.

If you feel guilty about throwing out the leftovers,
put them in the back of your refrigerator for five
days and then throw them out.

Redheads are extroverts.

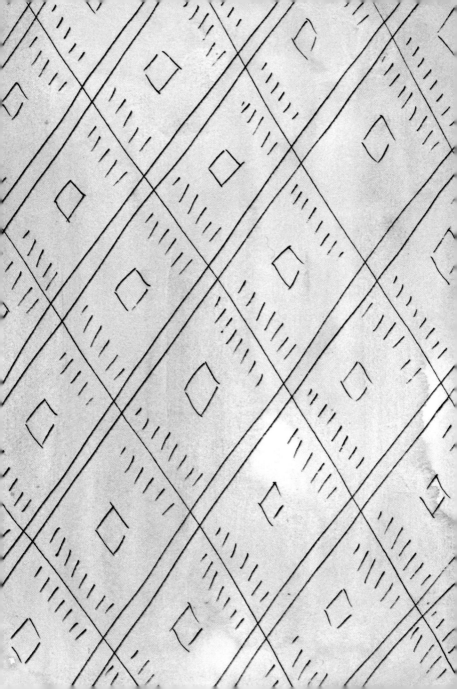

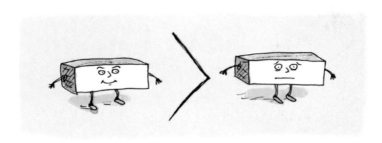

Sweet butter is better than salted butter.

Only Annie Oakley can pull off boots with short skirts.*

*This was pre-Uggs.

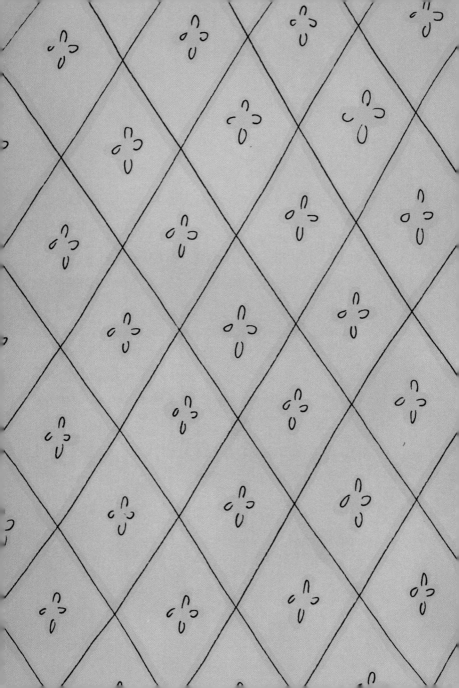

If you are writing a novel, I'll tell you what to do:
Don't make it boring.

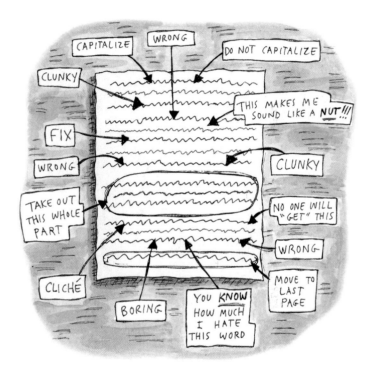

You should write my eulogy now so I can correct it.

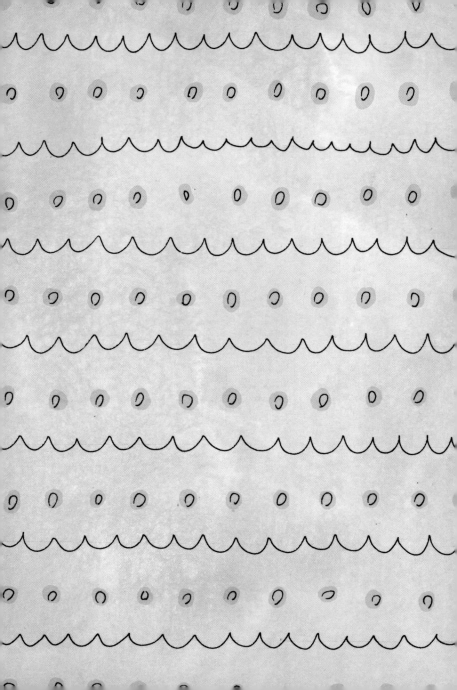

Show me now what you're going to
wear to my funeral so I can let you
know whether it's appropriate.

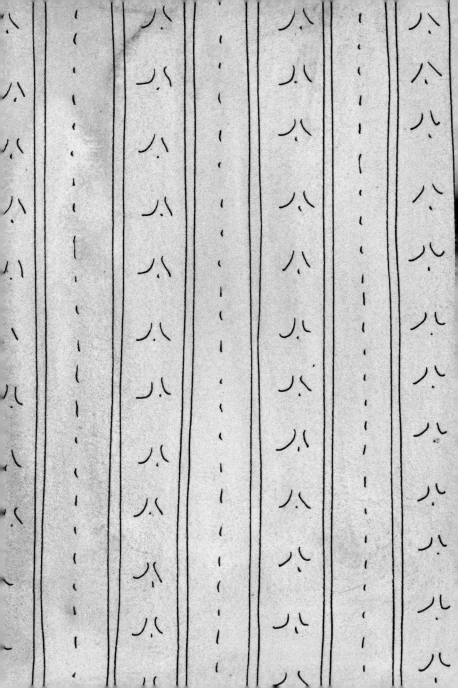

You only need to have one child,
but make sure it's the right one.

Babies who have colic grow up to have more confidence than easy babies because they receive more attention and are held a lot.

When it comes to raising children,
nothing beats bribery.

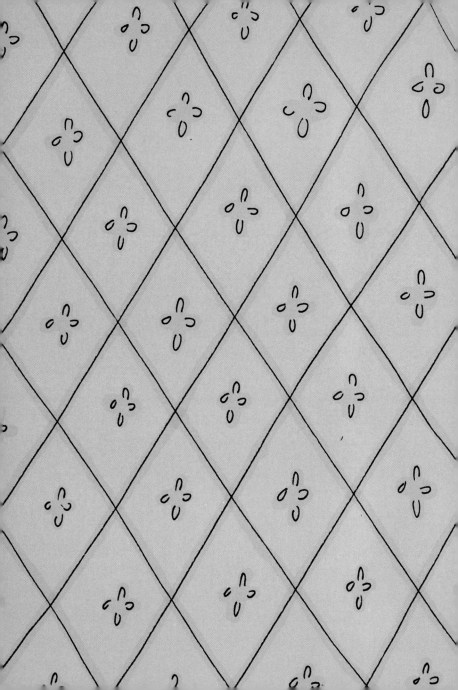

Keep the kitchen cabinets closed.

Never wear red and black together or
you will look like a drum majorette.

Plaids should not be based in white.

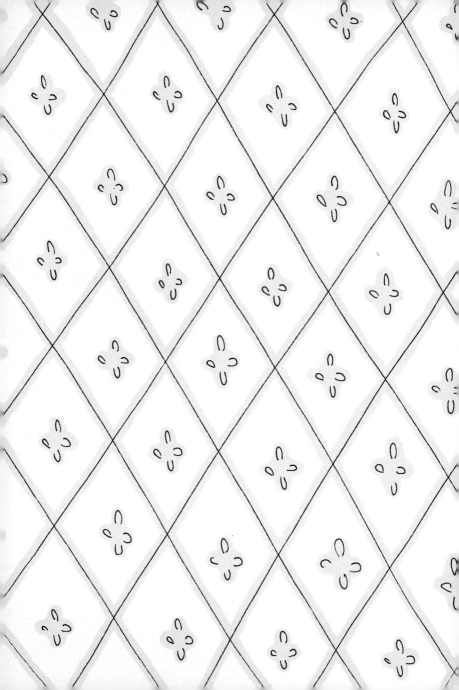

Everyone has a pre-determined number of footsteps to use up in a lifetime. It's reckless to exercise since you will only exhaust your quota sooner and die.

If you wear a white top with a black bottom to a party,
you will be mistaken for the caterer.

Mike says you can only have a Dalmatian whose spots
are symmetric and artfully placed.

Resist the temptation to buy clothes
on your skinniest day.

Your pocketbook should not have hardware unless the pocketbook is very, very, very expensive. If the hardware is genuine brass, you can't go wrong.

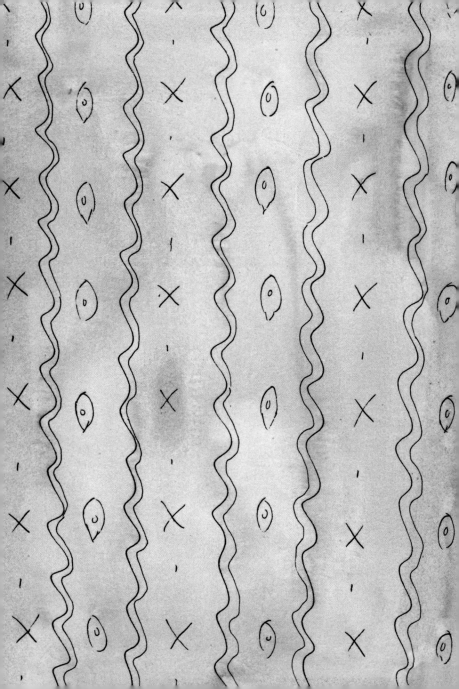

Everything would be better if they put me in
charge of naming the world.

Never serve salmon when entertaining. It is boring.

Religion is for kooks.

If you see me eating egg salad, you will
know the diagnosis is terminal.

Never put containers on the table.

Some people like meat well done, but they are wrong.

Portraits are better than landscapes.

Never buy a white car.

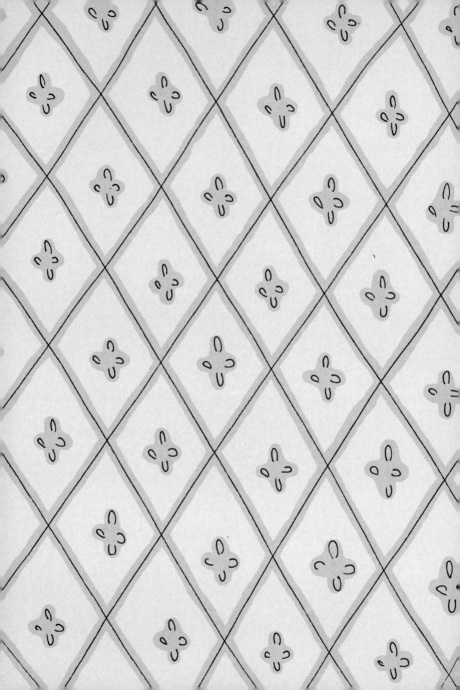

ABOUT THE AUTHOR

Patricia Marx has been contributing to *The New Yorker* since 1989. She is a former writer for *Saturday Night Live* and *Rugrats* and the author of several books. Marx was the first woman elected to *The Harvard Lampoon*.

Photograph © Alexandra Penney

ABOUT THE ILLUSTRATOR

Roz Chast has loved to draw cartoons since she was a child growing up in Brooklyn. She attended Rhode Island School of Design, majoring in Painting because it seemed more artistic. However, soon after graduating, she reverted to type and began drawing cartoons once again.

Photograph © Bill Franzen